THE AZTEC GOVERNMENT AND SOCIETY

HISTORY BOOKS BEST SELLERS

CHILDREN'S HISTORY BOOKS

Speedy Publishing LLC

40 E. Main St. #1156

Newark, DE 19711

www.speedypublishing.com

Copyright 2017

All Rights reserved. No part of this book may be reproduced or used in any way or form or by any means whether electronic or mechanical, this means that you cannot record or photocopy any material ideas or tips that are provided in this book.

In this book, we're going to talk about the Aztec government and society. So, let's get right to it!

THE AZTEC EMPIRE

The empire of the Aztecs was divided up into regions of government called city-states. At the core of each of these city-states was a large urban center where the government was situated. Although the empire did have a main ruler, he didn't interfere with the governing processes of the city-states. As long as the Aztec Emperor received his payment or tribute, he left them alone to govern themselves.

HUEY TLATOANI

The Aztecs had a government system that was similar to a kingdom where the king reigned over all the lands. Their ruler was the Huey Tlatoani, which when translated means "Great Speaker." He was the Aztec emperor and was the most powerful person in their civilization.

Motzume

The Aztecs believed that the gods had decided that he should rule. He was the decision-maker in terms of what wars they would fight and also the amounts of tributes from the lands they conquered.

When the Huey Tlatoani died, a new ruler was selected by a committee of nobles. Sometimes the new ruler was his son or another relative. If the emperor's brother was still living, he might be chosen if he was a natural leader.

ITZCÓATL
THE FOURTH AZTEC KING

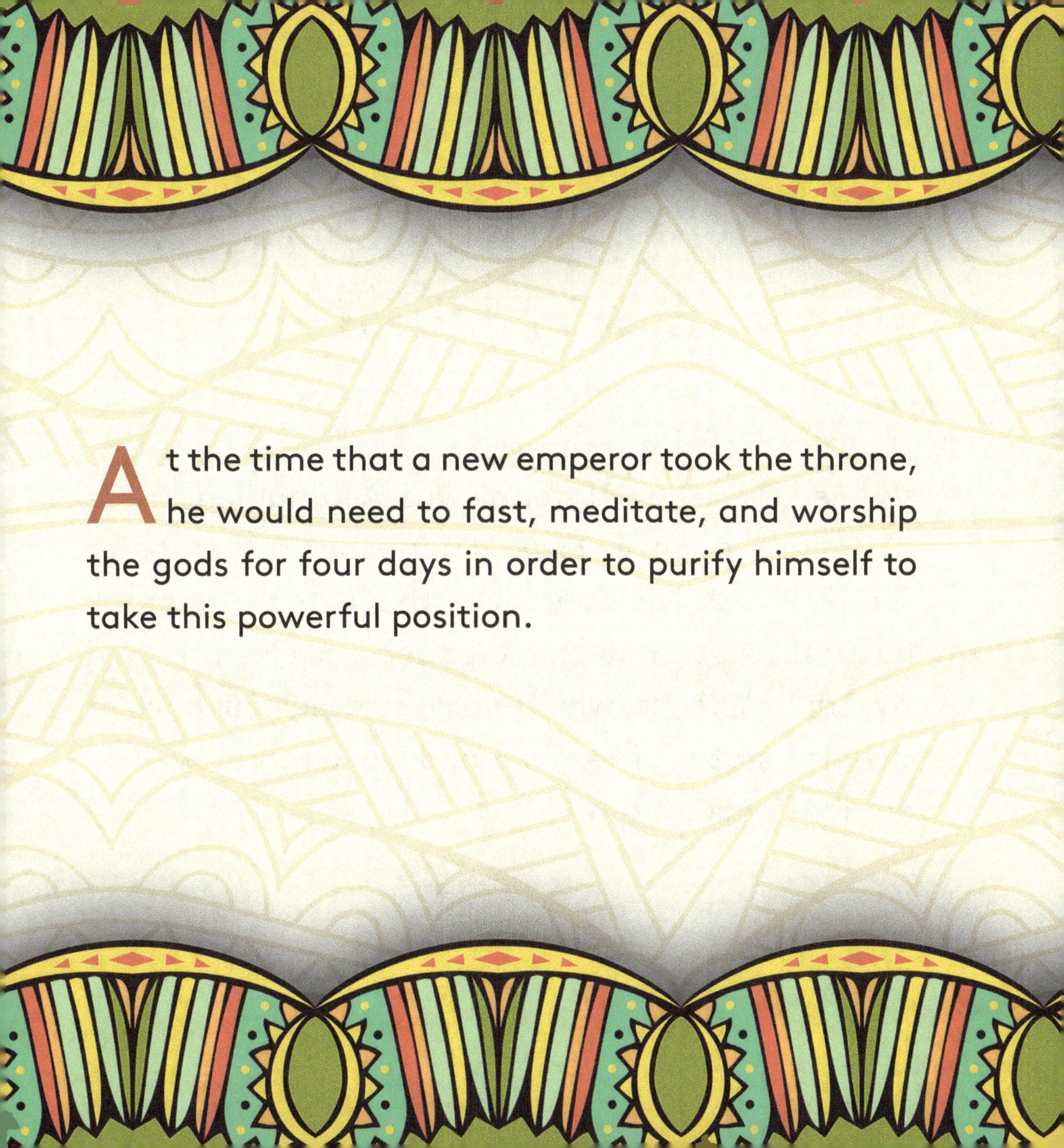

At the time that a new emperor took the throne, he would need to fast, meditate, and worship the gods for four days in order to purify himself to take this powerful position.

FAMOUS AZTEC EMPERORS

The first Huey Tlatoani was Acamapichtli. His reign began in 1375 AD and he was emperor for 19 years. The fourth of the Aztec emperors, Itzcoatl, overthrew the Tepanecs. He established the Triple Alliance, which was a strategic alliance of the city-states of Texcoco and Tlacopan as well as Mexico-Tenochtitlán.

ACAMAPICHTLI

MONTEZUMA

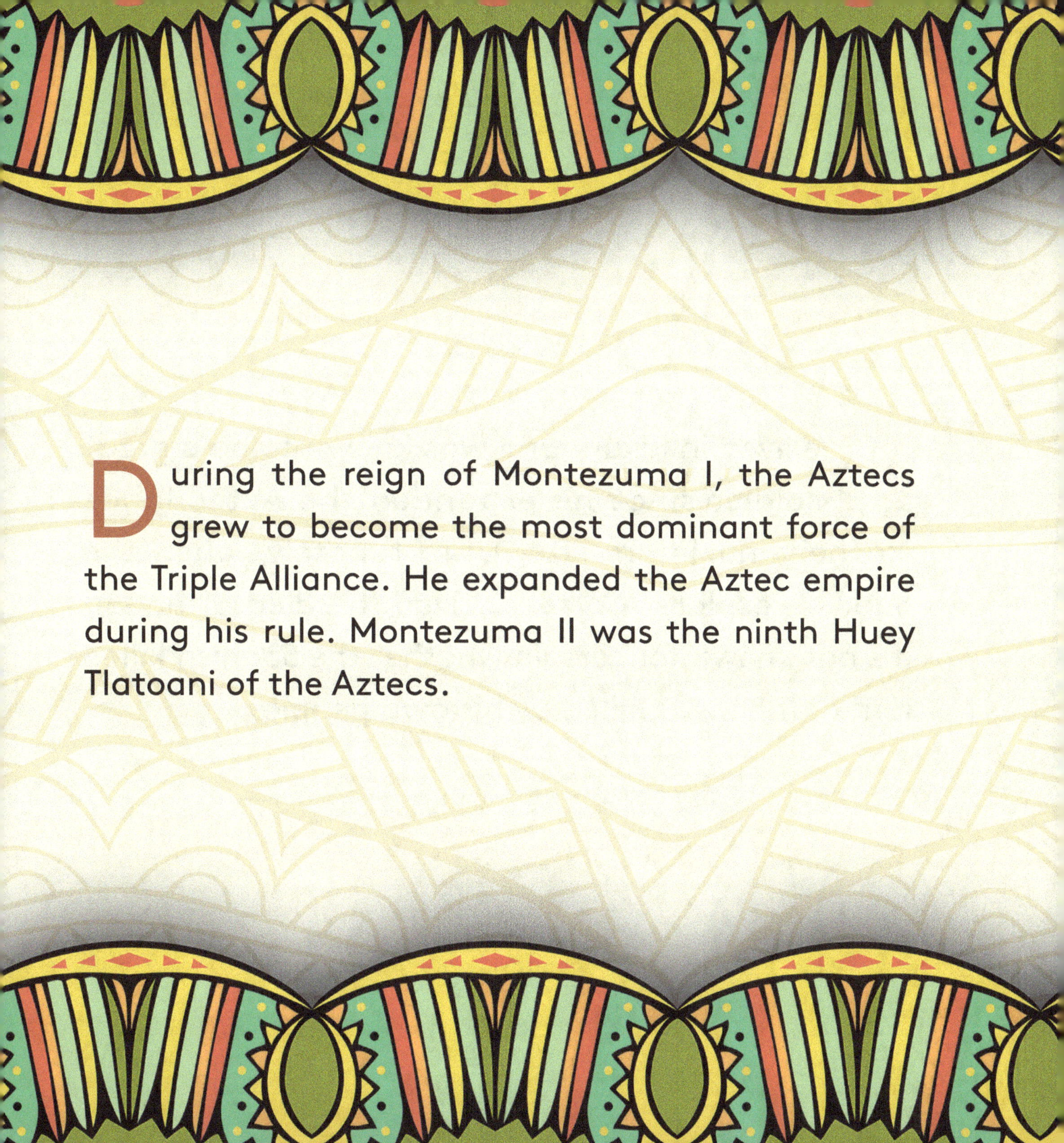

During the reign of Montezuma I, the Aztecs grew to become the most dominant force of the Triple Alliance. He expanded the Aztec empire during his rule. Montezuma II was the ninth Huey Tlatoani of the Aztecs.

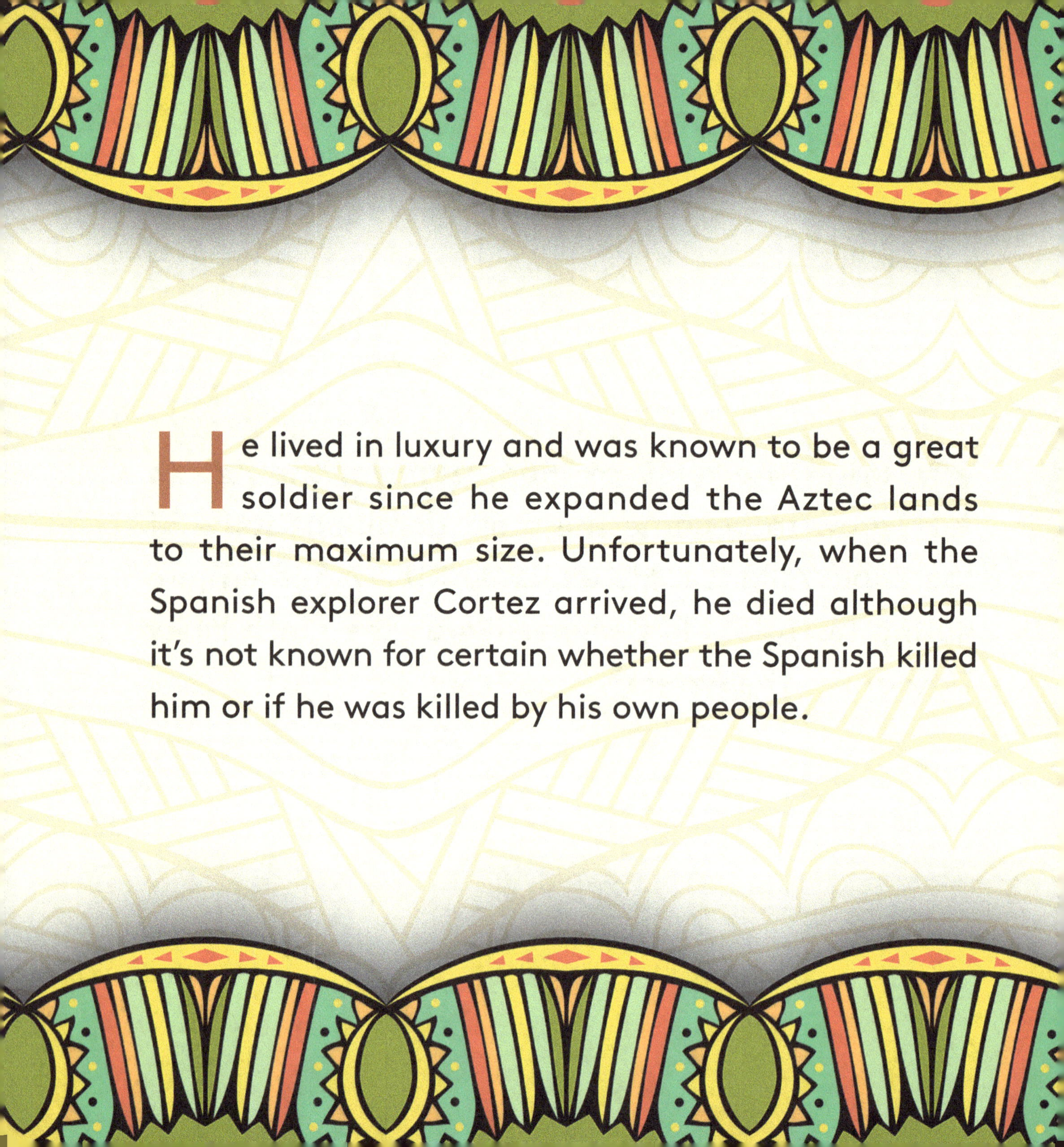

He lived in luxury and was known to be a great soldier since he expanded the Aztec lands to their maximum size. Unfortunately, when the Spanish explorer Cortez arrived, he died although it's not known for certain whether the Spanish killed him or if he was killed by his own people.

HERNÁN CORTÉS

CIHUACOATL STATUE

NEXT IN COMMAND

After the emperor, the Cihuacoatl was the second government official in the empire hierarchy. Although the word "Cihuacoatl" translates to "Female Serpent," this position was held by a man.

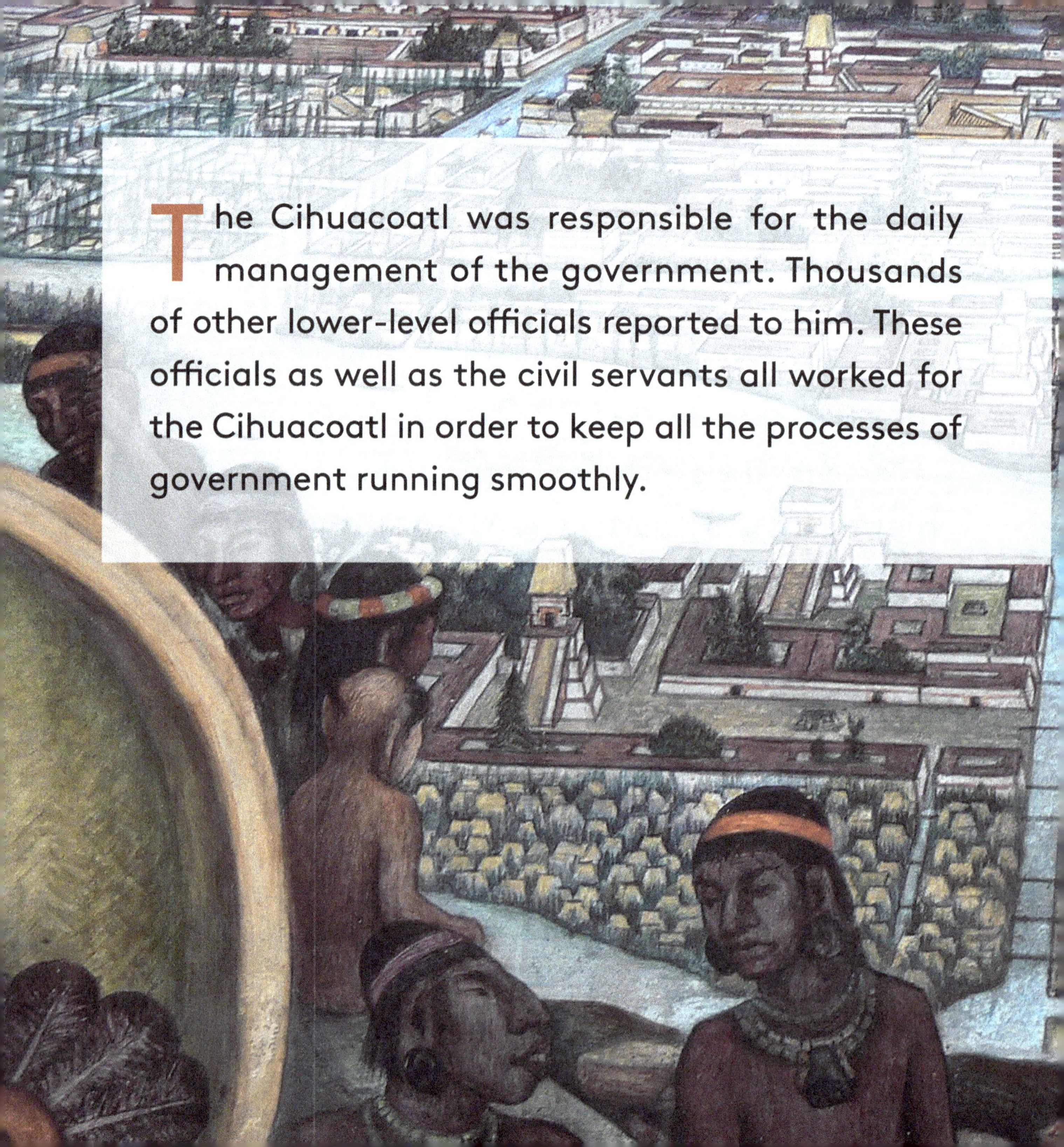

The Cihuacoatl was responsible for the daily management of the government. Thousands of other lower-level officials reported to him. These officials as well as the civil servants all worked for the Cihuacoatl in order to keep all the processes of government running smoothly.

Next in importance was a group of men called the "Council of Four." These men were powerful nobles and military generals who might be the next in line to take the throne should the emperor become sick or die.

MONTESUMA.

They were trusted consultants and gave the emperor advice. Since they were powerful in their own right, the emperor would work toward a consensus of opinion before making important decisions.

As in many other civilizations, government and religion were closely bound. The priests were considered to be important government officials because they were in charge of the religious rituals. They were also responsible for establishing the appropriate schools and teaching the young adults.

Chichen Itza

In addition to all these elite rulers, judges held positions of importance because they were responsible for the court system and military leaders were respected for their courage and bravery in war as well as their political skill.

THE CODE OF LAW

The Aztecs had very specific laws and the punishment for breaking the law was often severe. Depending on the nature of the crime, death was a common punishment. If not sentenced to death, a prisoner might be sold into slavery. Less severe, but still humiliating would be to have all the hair on your head shaved off.

Stealing and murder were considered crimes of the highest order. Property damage and drunkenness were not tolerated either. The court system was quite elaborate and there were varying court levels all the way to a "supreme court" that had the final say. If citizens were unhappy with a ruling they had received in a lesser court, they could kick it up to a higher-level court for review.

One very interesting law in the Aztec code calls for a "one-time pardon." If a citizen confessed a crime to his or her local priest, it would be absolved on the spot.

However, there were certain rules to abide by with this law. It was only accepted if the person confessed BEFORE being caught. Also, it was a one-time use only!

THE CITY OF TENOCHTITLN

The capital city of the Aztec empire was Tenochtitlán. The emperor lived there as did many of the most powerful elite. During the reign of Montezuma II when the Spanish explorers arrived, the population of the city was about a quarter of a million people. It was larger than London and some of the other large cities of Europe.

AZTEC SOCIETY

Aztec society was very structured. Just as it is in most countries, the family was the simplest unit. Marriage was a spiritual union as well as a physical one with its most important function being the bearing of children. Matchmakers arranged most of the marriages.

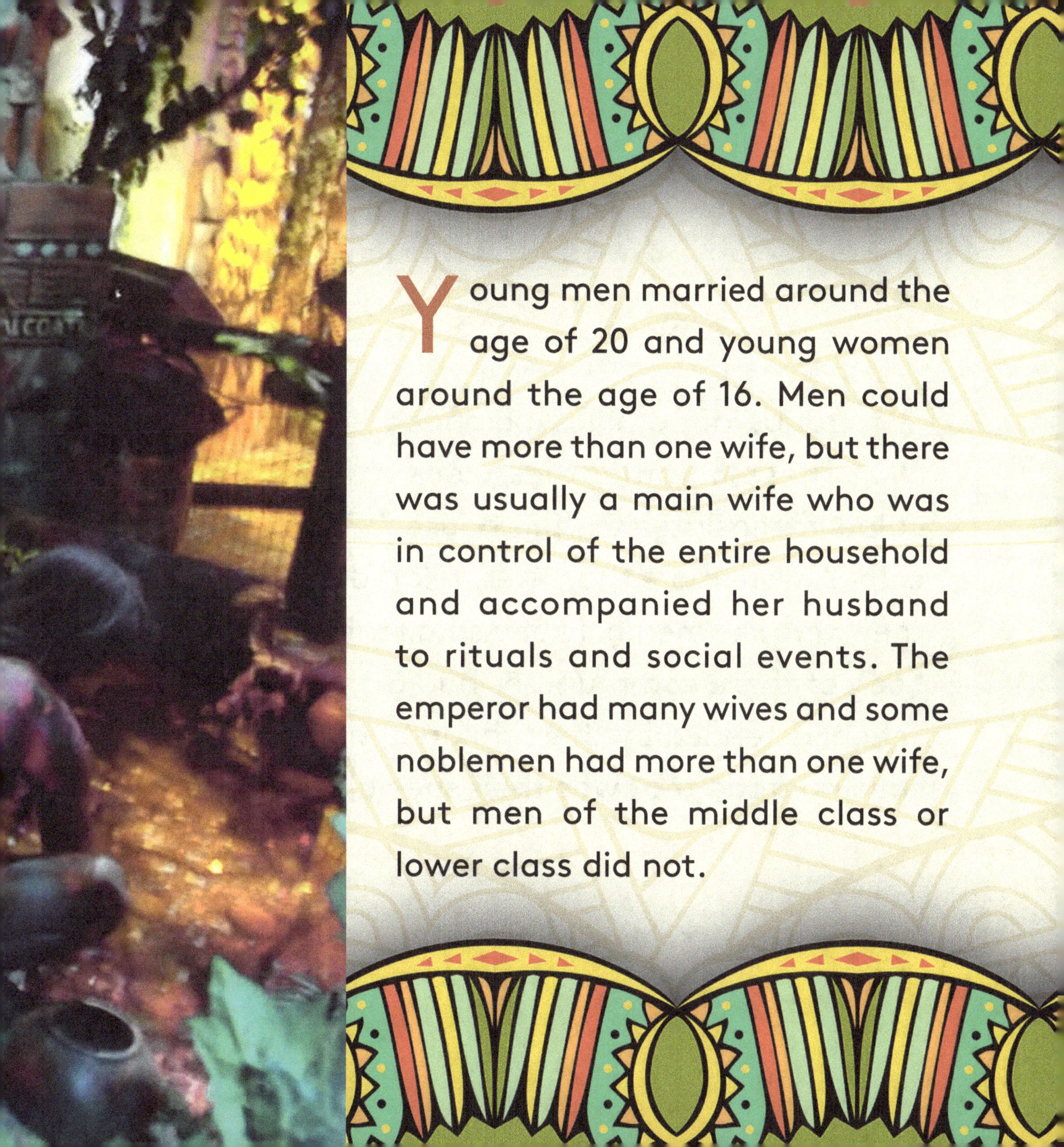

Young men married around the age of 20 and young women around the age of 16. Men could have more than one wife, but there was usually a main wife who was in control of the entire household and accompanied her husband to rituals and social events. The emperor had many wives and some noblemen had more than one wife, but men of the middle class or lower class did not.

CALPULLI

Groups of families belonged to communities. These communities were calpulli. The word calpulli translates to "big house." Families within a calpulli were more than likely related to each other so they were like members of a small tribe or family clan. Each of these communities had a chief ruler, a local school attended by their children, and sometimes a specific trade that was their specialization.

TENOCHTITLÁN

CITY-STATES

The city-states, also called Altepetl, were populated by many family clans. Each city-state had an urban area with surrounding farmlands. The largest of the city-states was Tenochtitlán, which was an amazing city built on an island. The emperor's palace was in Tenochtitlán and all the other city-states bowed down to him and paid him tribute.

SOCIETAL HIERARCHY

The king and his family were at the top of the social pyramid. After them, the remaining classes had power based on this order.

An aztec Ruler

TECUHTLI

This class was the group of rulers who were almost as important as the emperor. They helped him by ruling the other city-states just as he ruled the capital city-state. They were very rich and lived a life of luxury within their city-state's palaces. As long as they paid their tribute to the one emperor, they were allowed to run their city-states the way they pleased.

PIPILTIN

Next in social rank were the Pipiltin. They were the noblemen and their families. They held the high-ranking government, army, and religious positions. They were allowed to wear specific types of clothes to show their rank as well as adornments like feathers or gold. They also formed the committee council that gave advice to the emperor. It was believed that the Pipiltin were the ancestors of the Toltec people who came before the Aztecs.

A STATUE OF AN AZTEC NOBLE

POCHTECA

The Pochteca were an elite group of traveling merchants. They went on long journeys to obtain the luxury items wanted by the emperor, the Tecuhtli, and the Pipiltin. Because their jobs were so important, they were treated with the same level of respect as the nobility. They even had a god devoted specifically to them. His name was Yacetecuhtli and he protected them during their long journeys into sometimes hostile lands.

MACEHUALTIN

This group, the Macehualtin, were the ordinary people. They included farmers and fishermen as well as soldiers, merchants, and craftsmen. Later in their history this class split into two groups with the farmers and fishermen considered lower class than the others.

AZTEC ARMY

SLAVES

At the very bottom of the social ladder were the slaves. If you were the child of a slave, you weren't necessarily a slave. Aztecs became slaves if they owed debts they couldn't pay or they were accused of crimes and found guilty. Despite this, they had more rights than slaves in many other civilizations.

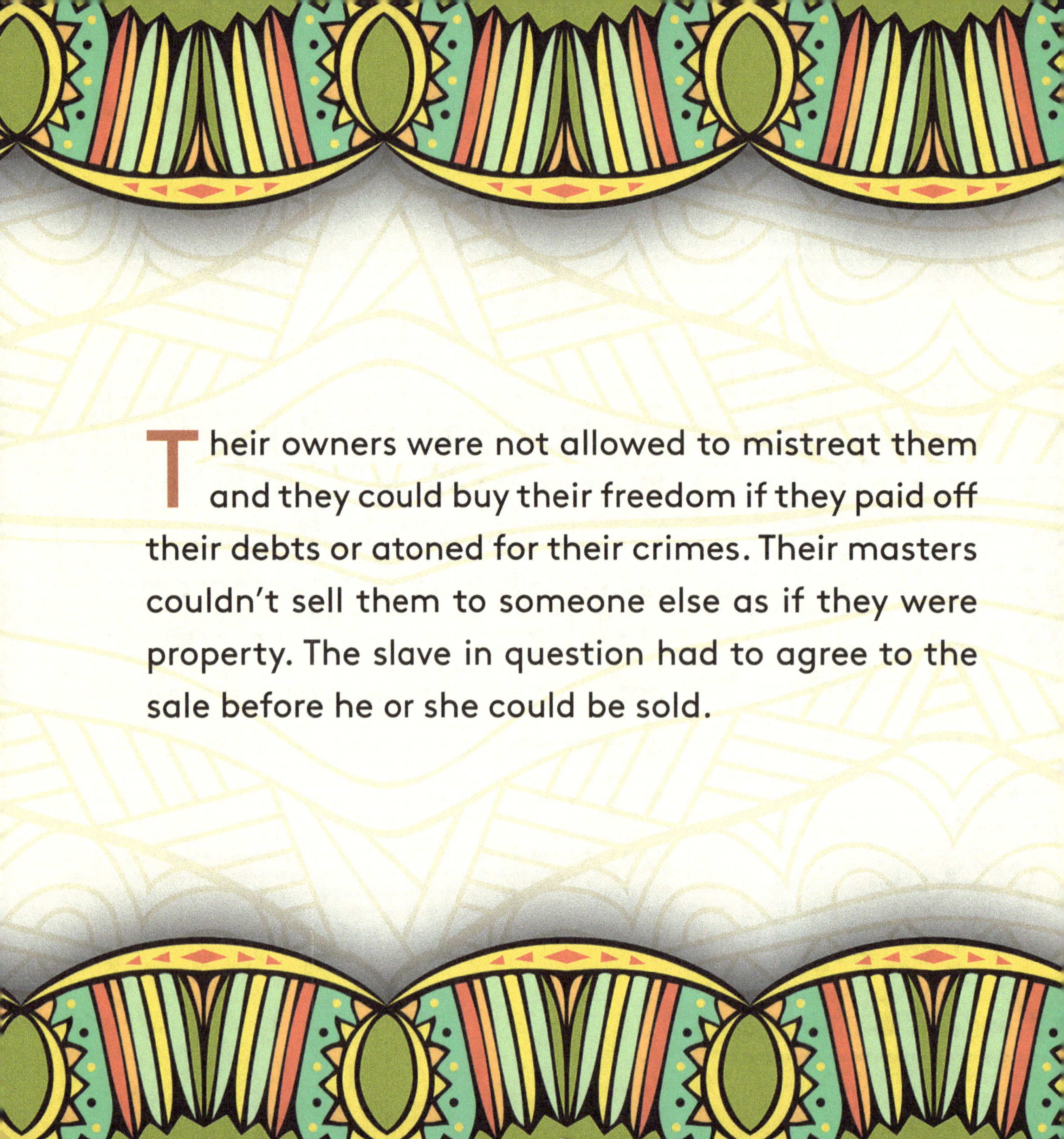

Their owners were not allowed to mistreat them and they could buy their freedom if they paid off their debts or atoned for their crimes. Their masters couldn't sell them to someone else as if they were property. The slave in question had to agree to the sale before he or she could be sold.

Man and slave relief

AZTEC PRIEST PERFORMING THE HUMAN SACRIFICE RITUAL

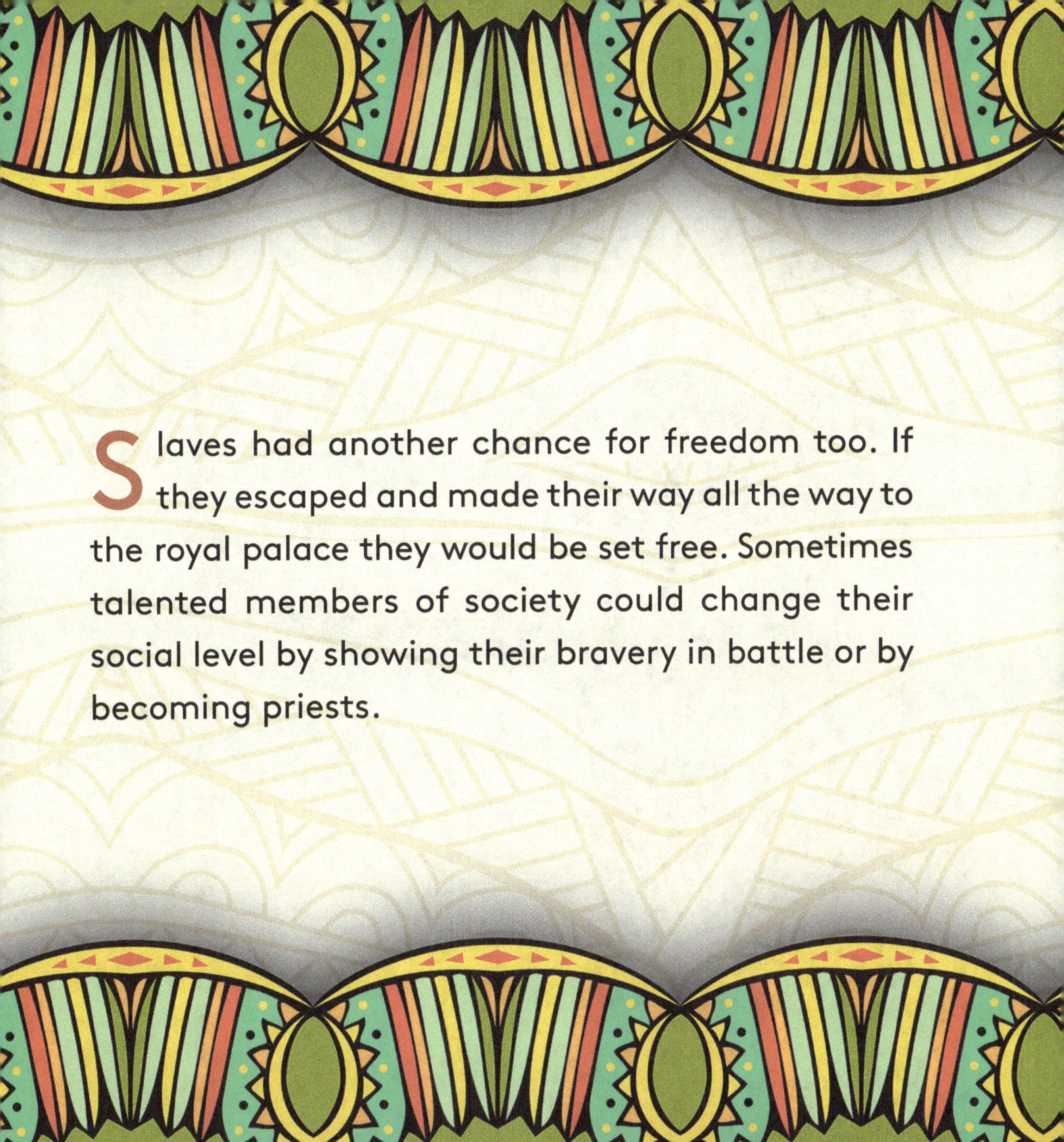

S laves had another chance for freedom too. If they escaped and made their way all the way to the royal palace they would be set free. Sometimes talented members of society could change their social level by showing their bravery in battle or by becoming priests.

Awesome! Now you know more about the government and society of the Aztec civilization. You can find more History books from Baby Professor by searching the website of your favorite book retailer.

Visit
BABY PROFESSOR
EDUCATION KIDS
www.BabyProfessorBooks.com
to download Free Baby Professor eBooks
and view our catalog of new and exciting
Children's Books

www.ingramcontent.com/pod-product-compliance
Lightning Source LLC
Chambersburg PA
CBHW080548180726
47999CB00022B/2684